A NATURE POEM FOR
EVERY SUMMER EVENING

A NATURE POEM FOR EVERY SUMMER EVENING

EDITED BY *Jane McMorland Hunter*

ILLUSTRATIONS BY *Jessamy Hawke*

BATSFORD

First published in the United Kingdom
in 2025 by
Batsford
43 Great Ormond Street
London
WC1N 3HZ

An imprint of B. T. Batsford Holdings Limited

ISBN 978 1 84994 861 6

A CIP catalogue record for this book is available from the
British Library.

10 9 8 7 6 5 4 3 2 1

Reproduction by Rival Colour Ltd, UK
Printed by Toppan Leefung Printing International Ltd, China

This book can be ordered direct from the publisher at
www.batsfordbooks.com, or try your local bookshop

Illustrations by Jessamy Hawke

CONTENTS

To Matilda, who came home. And to Mat
and Sarah, who helped. With all my love.

ABOUT THE EDITOR

Jane McMorland Hunter has compiled
anthologies for Batsford and the National Trust,
including collections on gardening, nature, food,
friendship, books, London, England and the First
World War. She also writes nature, gardening,
cookery, craft and children's books, and works at
Hatchard's Bookshop in Piccadilly, London. At
various times she has also worked as a gardener,
potter and quilter. She lives in London with a
small, grey tabby cat.

Introduction

One of the best ways to read nature poetry is
in the dappled light of a summer's evening.
The very length of summer days seems to give
us more time. Depending on where you are in
the world, it may not get dark until after
suppertime, perhaps even nearer to midnight.
This extra time is, of course, an illusion;
regardless of light or dark, each day is the same
length, but I cannot be the only person who is
taken in by a few extra hours of daylight.

Reading outside is another treat of summer
and, while a novel may absorb your attention
so completely that you do not notice your
surroundings, the comparative brevity of most
poems allows you to pause in your reading, look
around and take notice of the real world. The
world and the poem may not match, but that is
immaterial; it is the balance or contrast of the
two that matters.

There are scientific definitions and timings
for twilight and dusk but, from my point of view,
and I suspect that of many poets, it is a magical

time, neither day nor night, when the world seems gentler than in the harsh light of day. Thomas Gray's 'Elegy in a Country Churchyard' and Sara Teasdale's 'Dusk in June' were written roughly two hundred years apart, but both, and many poems in between, lyrically describe the evening.

If we are lucky, summer nights are gentle too. One of my favourite descriptions is Isaac Rosenberg's 'cooling rapture of the delicate starlight / Dropping from the night's blue walls in endless veils of loveliness', but there are also verses on the sea at night by David Austin and Matthew Arnold, William Wordsworth's 'soft half-moon' in London, Robert Browning's night-time meeting and Ethelwyn Wetherald's softly dimmed fields of dark.

Summer is the season with an abundance of flowers, in poetry as well as in the natural world. Foxgloves, marigolds, lilies and roses are followed by wild honeysuckle and sunflowers in poems from George Withers' seventeenth-century marigold in June to Laurence Binyon's neglected garden with weeds and flowers mingling at the end of August.

As summer progresses, many birds sing less, but they are still easy to spot, particularly the summer visitors. As are bats, butterflies and creatures such as glow-worms and crickets. See them in real life or read about them in verse; either is a perfect activity for a summer's evening.

To quote a very splendid children's book (*Dr Xargle's Book of Earth Weather* by Jeanne Willis and Tony Ross) the weather is nearly always 'too hot, too cold, too wet, too windy.' Haze, mist and wind all appear in verse but, as in everyday life, it is rain, or lack of it, that is the most conspicuous condition, from a cooling evening shower to a full-scale thunderstorm. We may complain about wet summers, but this is nothing new; in the eighteenth century John Codrington Bampfylde looked out onto 'the wistful train / of dripping poultry' on the farm and, nearly two hundred years later, Alice Meynell describes a rainy summer: 'rifled flowers are cold as ocean shells' and bees carrying 'their cold / wild honey to cold cells'.

Regardless of the weather, there is magic afoot in summer. William Shakespeare noticed it in *A Midsummer Night's Dream*, as did Rachel Field, who imagined harbourside hills as sleeping dragons. This collection also contains the opening verse of one of my favourite poems, George Macdonald's 'The Woods of Westermain', which dares the reader to enter the enchanted wood.

There are times in summer when the world seems to stand still, as famously described by Edward Thomas when an express-train unwontedly stops at a deserted station. These are the moments that spring has been leading up to, moments before summer tips down towards autumn. In the rush and bustle of daily life it is all too easy to miss these times. We blink, and suddenly the leaves are falling, the nights are drawing in and there is talk of winter. More than anything else, I believe that poetry can preserve these precious moments of summer.

Between the dusk of a summer night
    And the dawn of a summer day,
We caught at a mood as it passed in flight,
    And we bade it stoop and stay.

(From *Praeludium*, XXII by W. E. Henley)

JUNE

Balmy-sweet Summer Twilight

1ST JUNE

Foxgloves

The foxglove bells, with lolling tongue,
Will not reveal what peals were rung
In Faery, in Faery,
A thousand ages gone.
All the golden clappers hang
As if but now the changes rang;
Only from the mottled throat
Never any echoes float.
Quite forgotten, in the wood,
Pale, crowded steeples rise;
All the time that they have stood
None has heard their melodies.
Deep, deep in wizardry
All the foxglove belfries stand.
Should they startle over the land,
None would know what bells they be.
Never any wind can ring them,
Nor the great black bees that swing them –
Every crimson bell, down-slanted,
Is so utterly enchanted.

Mary Webb (1881–1927)

2ND JUNE

Thyrsis

A MONODY, TO COMMEMORATE THE AUTHOR'S FRIEND,
ARTHUR HUGH CLOUGH, WHO DIED AT FLORENCE, 1861
VERSES 6 AND 7

So, some tempestuous morn in early June,
 When the year's primal burst of bloom is o'er,
  Before the roses and the longest day –
 When garden-walks and all the grassy floor
  With blossoms red and white of fallen May
   And chestnut-flowers are strewn –
So have I heard the cuckoo's parting cry,
 From the wet field, through the vext garden-trees,
 Come with the volleying rain and tossing breeze:
The bloom is gone, and with the bloom go I!

Too quick despairer, wherefore wilt thou go?
 Soon will the high Midsummer pomps come on,
  Soon will the musk carnations break and swell,
 Soon shall we have gold-dusted snapdragon,
  Sweet-William with his homely cottage-smell,
   And stocks in fragrant blow;

Roses that down the alleys shine afar,
  And open, jasmine-muffled lattices,
  And groups under the dreaming garden-trees,
And the full moon, and the white evening-star.

Matthew Arnold (1822–1888)

3RD JUNE

The Nightingale and Glow-worm

LINES 1–26

A nightingale, that all day long
Had cheer'd the village with his song,
Nor yet at eve his note suspended,
Nor yet when eventide was ended,
Began to feel, as well he might,
The keen demands of appetite;
When, looking eagerly around,
He spied far off, upon the ground,
A something shining in the dark,
And knew the glow-worm by his spark;
So, stooping down from hawthorn top,
He thought to put him in his crop;
The worm, aware of his intent,
Harangued him thus right eloquent –
Did you admire my lamp, quoth he,
As much as I your minstrelsy,
You would abhor to do me wrong,
As much as I to spoil your song,
For 'twas the self-same pow'r divine
Taught you to sing, and me to shine,
That you with music, I with light,

Might beautify and cheer the night.
The songster heard his short oration,
And warbling out his approbation,
Releas'd him, as my story tells,
And found a supper somewhere else.

William Cowper (1731–1800)

4TH JUNE

Dusk in June

Evening, and all the birds
  In a chorus of shimmering sound
Are easing their hearts of joy
  For miles around.

The air is blue and sweet,
  The first few stars are white, –
Oh let me like the birds
  Sing before night.

Sara Teasdale (1884–1933)

5TH JUNE

Now Welcom Somer

FROM *THE PARLEMENT OF FOULES*, LINES 680–692

Now welcom somer, with thy sonne softe,
That hast this wintres weders over-shake,
And driven awey the longe nyghtes blake!

Saynt Valentyn, that art ful hy on-lofte; –
Thus singen smale foules for thy sake –
   Now welcom somer, with thy sonne softe,
   That hast this wintres weders over-shake.

Wel han they cause for to gladen ofte,
Sith ech of hem recovered hath his make;
Ful blisful may they singen whan they wake:
   Now welcom somer, with thy sonne softe
   That hast this wintres weders over-shake
   And driven awey the longe nyghtes blake.

Geoffrey Chaucer (c.1343–1400)

6TH JUNE

The Marigold

WHILST I THE SUN'S BRIGHT FACE MAY VIEW,
I WILL NO MEANER LIGHT PURSUE.

LINES 1–18

When with a serious musing I behold
The grateful and obsequious marigold;
How duly every morning, she displays
Her open breast when Titan spreads his rays;
How she observes him in his daily walk,
Still bending towards him her tender stalk;
How, when he down declines, she droops and mourns,
Bedewed (as 'twere) with tears, till he returns;
And how she vails her flow'rs when he is gone,
As if she scornèd to be lookèd on
By an inferior eye, or did contemn
To wait upon a meaner light than him.
When this I meditate, methinks the flowers
Have spirits far more generous than ours,
And give us fair examples to despise
The servile fawnings and idolatries
Wherewith we court these earthly things below,
Which merit not the service we bestow.

George Wither (1588–1667)

7TH JUNE

The Sea by Moonlight

Sleepless I lie
the long night through.

In the distance
the whispering of the sea,
in which we were
but this afternoon –
like two fishes.

No, the sea does not give up.
Her restless body moves,
even in the night,
while the clear-faced moon –
her lover –
sparkles in her belly,
and the land lies still in sleep.

David Austin (1926–2018)

8TH JUNE

To a Skylark

VERSES 1–7

Hail to thee, blithe Spirit!
  Bird thou never wert,
That from Heaven, or near it,
  Pourest thy full heart
In profuse strains of unpremeditated art.

Higher still and higher
  From the earth thou springest
Like a cloud of fire;
  The blue deep thou wingest,
And singing still dost soar, and soaring ever singest.

In the golden lightning
  Of the sunken sun,
O'er which clouds are bright'ning,
  Thou dost float and run;
Like an unbodied joy whose race is just begun.

The pale purple even
  Melts around thy flight;

Like a star of heaven
   In the broad daylight
Thou art unseen, but yet I hear thy shrill delight,

Keen as are the arrows
   Of that silver sphere,
Whose intense lamp narrows
   In the white dawn clear
Until we hardly see – we feel that it is there.

All the earth and air
   With thy voice is loud,
As, when night is bare,
   From one lonely cloud
The moon rains out her beams, and Heaven is overflowed.

What thou art we know not;
   What is most like thee?
From rainbow clouds there flow not
   Drops so bright to see
As from thy presence showers a rain of melody.

Percy Bysshe Shelley (1792–1822)

9TH JUNE

Brightening Fields

FROM *SUMMER, THE SEASONS*

From brightening fields of ether fair disclosed,
Child of the sun, refulgent Summer comes,
In pride of youth, and felt through Nature's depth:
He comes attended by the sultry hours,
And ever-fanning breezes, on his way;
While, from his ardent look, the turning Spring
Averts her blushful face; and earth, and skies,
All-smiling, to his hot domain leaves.
   Hence, let me haste into the mid-wood shade,
Where scarce a sunbeam wanders through the gloom;
And on the dark-green grass, beside the brink
Of haunted stream, that by the roots of oak
Rolls o'er the rocky channel, lie at large,
And sing the glories of the circling year.

James Thomson (1700–1748)

10TH JUNE

A Summer Twilight

It is a Summer twilight, balmy-sweet,
A twilight brighten'd by an infant moon,
Fraught with the fairest light of middle June;
The lonely garden echoes to my feet,
And hark! O hear I not the gentle dews,
Fretting the silent forest in his sleep?
Or does the stir of housing insects creep
Thus faintly on mine ear? Day's many hues
Waned with the paling light and are no more,
And none but reptile pinions beat the air:
The bat is hunting softly by my door,
And, noiseless as the snow-flake, leaves his lair;
O'er the still copses flitting here and there,
Wheeling the self-same circuit o'er and o'er.

Charles Tennyson Turner (1808–1879)

11ᵀᴴ JUNE

The Voice of Nature

I stand on the cliff and watch the veiled sun paling
  A silver field afar in the mournful sea,
The scourge of the surf, and plaintive gulls sailing
  At ease on the gale that smites the shuddering lea:
    Whose smile severe and chaste
  June never hath stirred to vanity, nor age defaced.
In lofty thought strive, O spirit, for ever:
In courage and strength pursue thine own endeavour.

Ah! if it were only for thee, thou restless ocean
  Of waves that follow and roar, the sweep of the tides;
Wer't only for thee, impetuous wind, whose motion
  Precipitate all o'errides, and turns, nor abides:
    For you sad birds and fair,
  Or only for thee, bleak cliff, erect in the air;
Then well could I read wisdom in every feature,
O well should I understand the voice of Nature.

But far away, I think, in the Thames valley,
   The silent river glides by flowery banks:
And birds sing sweetly in branches that arch an alley
   Of cloistered trees, moss-grown in their ancient ranks:
      Where if a light air stray,
   'Tis laden with hum of bees and scent of may.
Love and peace be thine, O spirit, for ever:
Serve thy sweet desire: despise endeavour.

And if it were only for thee, entrancèd river,
   That scarce dost rock the lily on her airy stem,
Or stir a wave to murmur, or a rush to quiver;
   Wer't but for the woods, and summer asleep in them:
      For you my bowers green,
   My hedges of rose and woodbine, with walks between,
Then well could I read wisdom in every feature,
O well should I understand the voice of Nature.

Robert Bridges (1844–1930)

12TH JUNE

The Hills

Sometimes I think the hills
That loom across the harbor
Lie there like sleeping dragons,
Crouched one above another.
With trees for tufts of fur
Growing all up and down
The ridges and humps of their backs,
And orange cliffs for claws
Dipped in the sea below.
Sometimes a wisp of smoke
Rises out of the hollows,
As if in their dragon sleep
They dreamed of strange old battles.

What if the hills should stir
Some day and stretch themselves,
Shake off the clinging trees
And all the clustered houses?

Rachel Field (1894–1942)

13TH JUNE

The Woods of Westermain

Enter these enchanted woods,
　　You who dare
Nothing harms beneath the leaves
More than waves a swimmer cleaves.
Toss your heart up with the lark,
Foot at pace with mouse and worm,
　　Fair you fare.
Only at the dread of dark
Quaver, and they quit their form:
Thousand eyeballs under hoods
　　Have you by the hair.
Enter these enchanted woods,
　　You who dare.

George Meredith (1828–1909)

14TH JUNE

Renascence

LINES 1–26

All I could see from where I stood
Was three long mountains and a wood;
I turned and looked another way,
And saw three islands in a bay.
So with my eyes I traced the line
Of the horizon, thin and fine,
Straight around till I was come
Back to where I'd started from;
And all I saw from where I stood
Was three long mountains and a wood.
Over these things I could not see;
These were the things that bounded me;
And I could touch them with my hand,
Almost, I thought, from where I stand.
And all at once things seemed so small
My breath came short, and scarce at all.
But, sure, the sky is big, I said;
Miles and miles above my head;
So here upon my back I'll lie

And look my fill into the sky.
And so I looked, and, after all,
The sky was not so very tall.
The sky, I said, must somewhere stop,
And – sure enough! – I see the top!
The sky, I thought, is not so grand;
I 'most could touch it with my hand!

Edna St Vincent Millay (1892–1950)

15TH JUNE

The Setting Sun

This scene, how beauteous to the musing mind
That now swift slides from my enchanted view
The Sun sweet setting yon far hills behind
In other worlds his Visits to renew
What spangling glories all around him shine
What nameless colours cloudless and serene
(A heavnly prospect brightest in decline)
Attend his exit from this lovely scene –
– So sets the christians sun in glories clear
So shines his soul at his departure here
No clouding doubts nor misty fears arise
To dim hopes golden rays of being forgiven
His sun sweet setting in the clearest skyes
In safe assurance wings the soul to heaven.

John Clare (1793–1864)

16TH JUNE

Dover Beach

The sea is calm to-night.
The tide is full, the moon lies fair
Upon the straits; – on the French coast the light
Gleams and is gone; the cliffs of England stand,
Glimmering and vast, out in the tranquil bay.
Come to the window, sweet is the night air!
Only, from the ling line of spray
Where the sea meets the moon-blanch'd land,
Listen! you hear the grating roar
Of pebbles which the waves draw back, and fling,
At their return, up the high strand,
Begin, and cease, and then again begin,
With tremulous cadence slow, and bring
The eternal note of sadness in.

Sophocles long ago
Heard it on the Ægæan, and it brought
Into his mind the turbid ebb and flow
Of human misery; we
Find also in the sound a thought,
Hearing it by this distant northern sea.

The Sea of Faith
Was once, at the full, and round earth's shore
Lay like the folds of a bright girdle furl'd.
But now I only hear
Its melancholy, long, withdrawing roar,
Retreating, to the breath
Of the night-wind, down the vast edges drear
And naked shingles of this world.

Ah, love, let us be true
To one another! for the world, which seems
To lie before us like a land of dreams,
So various, so beautiful, so new,
Hath really neither joy, nor love, nor light,
Nor certitude, nor peace, nor help for pain;
And we are here as on a darkling plain
Swept with confused alarms of struggle and flight,
Where ignorant armies clash by night.

Matthew Arnold (1822–1888)

17TH JUNE

The Lily and the Rose

The nymph must lose her female friend
  If more admir'd than she –
But where will fierce contention end
  If flow'rs can disagree?

Within the garden's peaceful scene
  Appear'd two lovely foes,
Aspiring to the rank of queen –
  The Lily and the Rose.

The Rose soon redden'd into rage,
  And, swelling with disdain,
Appeal'd to many a poet's page
  To prove her right to reign.

The Lily's height bespoke command –
  A fair imperial flow'r,
She seemed design'd for Flora's hand,
  The sceptre of her pow'r.

This civil bick'ring and debate
  The goddess chanc'd to hear,
And flew to save, ere yet too late,
  The pride of the parterre. –

Your's is, she said, the nobler hue,
  And your's the statelier mien,
And, till a third surpasses you,
  Let each be deem'd a queen.

Thus, sooth'd and reconcil'd, each seeks
  The fairest British fair,
The seat of empire is her cheeks,
  They reign united there.

William Cowper (1731–1800)

18TH JUNE

A Waterpiece

The wild-rose bush lets loll
Her sweet-breathed petals on the pearl-smoothed pool,
The bream-pool overshadowed with the cool
Of oaks where myriad mumbling wings patrol.
There the live dimness burrs with droning glees
Of hobby-horses with their starting eyes
And violet humble-bees and dizzy flies;
That from the dewsprings drink the honeyed lees.

Up the slow stream the immemorial bream
(For when had Death dominion over them?)
Through green pavilions of ghost leaf and stem,
A conclave of blue shadows in a dream,
Glide on; idola that forgotten plan,
Incomparably wise, the doom of man.

Edmund Blunden (1896–1974)

19TH JUNE

Moonrise, June 19, 1876

I awoke in the midsummer not-to-call night, |
  in the white and the walk of the morning:
The móon, dwíndled and thínned to the fringe |
  of a fingernail héld to the cándle,
Or páring of páradisáïcal frúit, | lóvely in wáning
  but lústreless,
Stepped from the stool, drew back from the
  barrow, | of dark Maenefa the mountain;
A cusp still clasped him, a fluke yet fanged him, |
  entangled him, not quit utterly.
This was the prized, the desirable sight, |
  unsought, presented so easily,
Parted me leaf and leaf, divided me, | eyelid and
  eyelid of slumber.

Gerard Manley Hopkins (1844–1889)

20TH JUNE

Adlestrop

Yes. I remember Adlestrop –
The name, because one afternoon
Of heat the express-train drew up there
Unwontedly. It was late June.

The steam hissed. Someone cleared his throat.
No one left and no one came
On the bare platform. What I saw
Was Adlestrop – only the name

And willows, willow-herb, and grass,
And meadowsweet, and haycocks dry,
No whit less still and lonely fair
Than the high cloudlets in the sky.

And for that minute a blackbird sang
Close by, and round him, mistier,
Farther and farther, all the birds
Of Oxfordshire and Gloucestershire.

Edward Thomas (1878–1917)

21ˢᵀ JUNE

Endymion

A thing of beauty is a joy for ever:
Its loveliness increases; it will never
Pass into nothingness; but will still keep
A bower quiet for us, and a sleep
Full of sweet dreams, and health, and quiet breathing.
Therefore, on every morrow, we are wreathing
A flowery band to bind us to the earth,
Spite of despondence, of the inhuman dearth
Of noble natures, of the gloomy days,
Of all the unhealthy and o'er-darkened ways
Made for our searching: yes, in spite of all,
Some shape of beauty moves away the pall
From our dark spirits. Such the sun, the moon,
Trees old, and young, sprouting a shady boon
For simple sheep; and such are daffodils
With the green world they live in; and clear rills
That for themselves a cooling covert make
'Gainst the hot season; the mid forest brake,
Rich with a sprinkling of fair musk-rose blooms:
And such too is the grandeur of the dooms

We have imagined for the mighty dead;
All lovely tales that we have heard or read:
An endless fountain of immortal drink,
Pouring unto us from heaven's brink.

   Nor do we merely feel these essences
For one short hour; no, even as the trees
That whisper round a temple become soon
Dear as the temple's self, so does the moon,
The passion poesy, glories infinite,
Haunt us till they become a cheering light
Unto our souls and bound to us so fast,
That, whether there be shine, or gloom o'ercast,
They always must be with us, or we die.

John Keats (1795–1821)

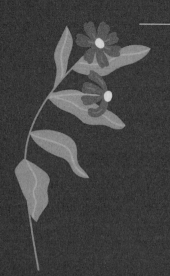

22ND JUNE

The Sundew

A little marsh-plant, yellow green,
And pricked at lip with tender red.
Tread close, and either way you tread
Some faint black water jets between
Lest you should bruise the curious head.

A live thing maybe; who shall know?
The summer knows and suffers it;
For the cool moss is thick and sweet
Each side, and saves the blossom so
That it lives out the long June heat.

The deep scent of the heather burns
About it; breathless though it be,
Bow down and worship; more than we
Is the least flower whose life returns,
Least weed renascent in the sea.

We are vexed and cumbered in earth's sight
With wants, with many memories;
These see their mother what she is,
Glad-growing, till August leave more bright
The apple-coloured cranberries.

Wind blows and bleaches the strong grass,
Blown all one way to shelter it
From trample of strayed kine, with feet
Felt heavier than the moorhen was,
Strayed up past patches of wild wheat.

You call it sundew: how it grows,
If with its colour it have breath,
If life taste sweet to it, if death
Pain its soft petal, no man knows:
Man has no sight or sense that saith.

My sundew, grown of gentle days,
In these green miles the spring begun
Thy growth ere April had half done
With the soft secret of her ways
Or June made ready for the sun.

O red-lipped mouth of marsh-flower,
I have a secret halved with thee.
The name that is love's name to me
Thou knowest, and the face of her
Who is my festival to see.

The hard sun, as thy petals knew,
Coloured the heavy moss-water:
Thou wert not worth green midsummer
Nor fit to live to August blue,
O sundew, not remembering her.

Algernon Charles Swinburne (1837–1909)

23RD JUNE

Night

FROM *SONGS OF INNOCENCE*

VERSES 1 AND 2

The sun descending in the west,
The evening star does shine;
The birds are silent in their nest.
And I must seek for mine.
The moon, like a flower
In heaven's high bower,
With silent delight
Sits and smiles on the night.

Farewell, green fields and happy groves,
Where flocks have took delight:
Where lambs have nibbled, silent moves
The feet of angels bright;
Unseen they pour blessing,
And joy without ceasing,
On each bud and blossom,
And each sleeping bosom.

William Blake (1757–1827)

24TH JUNE

Sonnet 98

From you have I been absent in the spring,
When proud-pied April, dressed in all his trim,
Hath put a spirit of youth in everything,
That heavy Saturn laughed and leaped with him,
Yet nor the lays of birds, nor the sweet smell
Of different flowers in odour and in hue,
Could make me any summer's story tell,
Or from their proud lap pluck them where they grew.
Nor did I wonder at the lily's white,
Nor praise the deep vermilion in the rose;
They were but sweet, but figures of delight,
Drawn after you, you pattern of all those.
  Yet seemed it winter still, and, you away,
  As with your shadow I with these did play.

William Shakespeare (1564–1616)

25TH JUNE

The Sun Has Long Been Set

The sun has long been set,
   The stars are out by twos and threes,
The little birds are piping yet
   Among the bushes and the trees;
There's a cuckoo, and one or two thrushes,
And a far-off wind that rushes,
And a sound of water that gushes,
And the cuckoo's sovereign cry
Fills all the hollow of the sky.
   Who would 'go parading'
In London, 'and masquerading,'
On such a night of June
With that beautiful soft half-moon,
And all these innocent blisses?
On such a night as this is!

William Wordsworth (1770–1850)

26TH JUNE

The Fields of Dark

The wreathing vine within the porch
  Is in the heart of me,
The roses that the noondays scorch
  Burn on in memory;
Alone at night I quench the light,
  And without star or spark
The grass and trees press to my knees,
  And flowers throng the dark.

The leaves that loose their hold at noon
  Drop on my face like rain,
And in the watches of the moon
  I feel them fall again.
By day I stray how far away
  To stream and wood and steep,
But on my track they all come back
  To haunt the vale of sleep.

The fields of light are clover-brimmed,
  Or grassed or daisy-starred;
The fields of dark are softly dimmed,
  And safety twilight-barred;
But in the gloom that fills my room
  I cannot fail to mark
The grass and trees about my knees,
  The flowers in the dark.

Ethelwyn Wetherald (1857–1940)

27TH **JUNE**

The Vision of Sir Launfal

And what is so rare as a day in June?
   Then, if ever, come perfect days;
Then Heaven tries earth if it be in tune,
   And over it softly her warm ear lays:
Whether we look, or whether we listen,
We hear life murmur, or see it glisten;
Every clod feels a stir of might,
   An instinct within it that reaches and towers,
And, groping blindly above it for light,
   Climbs to a soul in grass and flowers;
The flush of life may well be seen
   Thrilling back over hills and valleys;
The cowslip startles in meadows green,
   The buttercup catches the sun in its chalice,
And there's never a leaf nor a blade too mean
   To be some happy creature's palace;
The little bird sits at his door in the sun,
   Atilt like a blossom among the leaves,
And lets his illumined being o'errun

    With the deluge of summer it receives;
His mate feels the eggs beneath her wings,
And the heart in her dumb breast flutters and sings;
He sings to the wide world, and she to her nest, –
In the nice ear of Nature which song is the best?

James Russell Lowell (1819–1891)

28TH JUNE

I Love Flowers

SIBYLLA FROM *DEATH'S JEST-BOOK*, ACT V, SCENE III

I love flowers too; not for a young girl's reason,
But because these brief visitors to us
Rise yearly from the neighbourhood of the dead,
To show us how far fairer and more lovely
Their world is; and return thither again,
Like parting friends that beckon us to follow,
And lead the way silent and smilingly.
Fair is the season when they come to us,
Unfolding the delights of that existence
Which is below us: 'tis the time of spirits,
Who with the flowers, and, like them, leave their graves:
But when the earth is sealed, and none dare come
Upwards to cheer us, and man's left alone,
We have cold, cutting winter.

Thomas Lovell Beddoes (1803–1849)

29TH JUNE

To the Grasshopper and the Cricket

Green little vaulter in the sunny grass,
Catching your heart up at the feel of June,
Sole voice that's heard amidst the lazy noon,
When even the bees lag at the summoning brass,
And you, warm little housekeeper, who class
With those who think the candles come too soon,
Loving the fire, and with your tricksome tune
Nick the glad silent moments as they pass;
Oh sweet and tiny cousins, that belong
One to the fields, the other to the hearth,
Both have your sunshine; both, though small, are strong
At your clear hearts; and both were sent on earth
To sing in thoughtful ears this natural song –
Indoors and out, summer and winter, Mirth.

Leigh Hunt (1784–1859)

30TH JUNE

Summer

Winter is cold-hearted,
    Spring is yea and nay,
Autumn is a weathercock
    Blown every way:
Summer days for me
    When every leaf is on its tree;

When Robin's not a beggar,
    And Jenny Wren's a bride,
And larks hang singing, singing, singing,
    Over the wheat-fields wide,
And anchored lilies ride,
    And the pendulum spider
Swings from side to side;

And blue-black beetles transact business,
    And gnats fly in a host,
And furry caterpillars hasten
    That no time be lost,
And moths grow fat and thrive,
    And ladybirds arrive.

Before green apples blush,
     Before green nuts embrown,
Why, one day in the country
     Is worth a month in town;
     Is worth a day and a year
Of the dusty, musty, lag-last fashion
     That days drone elsewhere.

Christina Rossetti (1830–1894)

JULY

Each Daisy Stands Like a Star

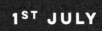

1ST JULY

The Thistle's Grown Aboon the Rose

VERSE 1

Full white the Bourbon lily blows,
And farer haughty England's rose.
Nor shall unsung the symbol smile,
Green Ireland, of thy lovely isle.
In Scotland grows a warlike flower,
Too rough to bloom in lady's bower;
His crest, when high the soldier bears,
And spurs his courser on the spears.
O, there it blossoms – there it blows –
The thistle's grown aboon the rose.

Allan Cunningham (1784–1842)

2ND JULY

The Brook

Seated once by a brook, watching a child
Chiefly that paddled, I was thus beguiled.
Mellow the blackbird sang and sharp the thrush
Not far off in the oak and hazel brush,
Unseen. There was a scent like honeycomb
From mugwort dull. And down upon the dome
Of the stone the cart-horse kicks against so oft
A butterfly alighted. From aloft
He took the heat of the sun, and from below.
On the hot stone he perched contented so,
As if never a cart would pass again
That way; as if I were the last of men
And he the first of insects to have earth
And sun together and to know their worth.
I was divided between him and the gleam,
The motion, and the voices, of the stream,
The waters running frizzled over gravel,
That never vanish and for ever travel.
A grey flycatcher silent on a fence
And I sat as if we had been there since
The horseman and the horse lying beneath
The fir-tree-covered barrow on the heath,

The horseman and the horse with silver shoes,
Galloped the downs last. All that I could lose
I lost. And then the child's voice raised the dead.
'No one's been here before' was what she said
And what I felt, yet never should have found
A word for, while I gathered sight and sound.

Edward Thomas (1878-1917)

3RD JULY

Twilight-Piece

The golden river-reach afar
  Kisses the golden skies of even,
And there's the first faint lover's star
  Alight along the walls of heaven.

The river murmurs to the boughs,
  The boughs make music each to each,
And still an amorous west wind soughs
  And loiters down the lonesome reach.

And here on the slim arch that spans
  The rippling stream, in dark outline,
You see the poor old fisherman's
  Bowed form and patient rod and line.

A picture better than all art,
  Since none could catch that sunset stain,
Or set in the soft twilight's heart
  This small strange touch of human pain!

Victor Plarr (1863–1929)

4TH JULY

Wild Honeysuckle

Fair flower, that dost so comely grow,
Hid in this silent, dull retreat,
Untouched thy honied blossoms blow,
Unseen thy little branches greet:
  No roving foot shall crush thee here,
  No busy hand provoke a tear.

By Nature's self in white arrayed,
She bade thee shun the vulgar eye,
And planted here the guardian shade,
And sent soft waters murmuring by;
  Thus quietly thy summer goes,
  Thy days declining to repose.

Smit with those charms, that must decay,
I grieve to see your future doom;
They died – nor were those flowers more gay,
The flowers that did in Eden bloom;
  Unpitying frosts and Autumn's power
  Shall leave no vestige of this flower.

From morning suns and evening dews
At first thy little being came;
If nothing once, you nothing lose,
For when you die you are the same;
 The space between is but an hour,
 The frail duration of flower.

Philip Freneau (1752–1832)

5TH JULY

Ocean, an Ode

VERSES 1 AND 2

Sweet rural scene!
Of flocks and green!
At careless ease my limbs are spread;
All nature still
But yonder rill;
And listening pines not o'er my head:

In prospect wide,
The boundless tide!
Waves cease to foam, and winds to roar;
Without a breeze,
The curling seas
Dance on, in measure, to the shore.

Edward Young (1683–1765)

6TH JULY

In Summer

Oh, summer has clothed the earth
In a cloak from the loom of the sun!
And a mantle, too, of the skies' soft blue,
And a belt where the rivers run.

And now for the kiss of the wind,
And the touch of the air's soft hands,
With the rest from strife and the heat of life,
With the freedom of lakes and lands.

I envy the farmer's boy
Who sings as he follows the plow;
While the shining green of the young blades lean
To the breezes that cool his brow.

He sings to the dewy morn,
No thought of another's ear;
But the song he sings is a chant for kings
And the whole wide world to hear.

He sings of the joys of life,
Of the pleasures of work and rest,
From an o'erfull heart, without aim or art;
'Tis a song of the merriest.

O ye who toil in the town,
And ye who moil in the mart,
Hear the artless song, and your faith made strong
Shall renew your joy of heart.

Oh, poor were the worth of the world
If never a song were heard, –
If the sting of grief had no relief,
And never a heart were stirred.

So, long as the streams run down,
And as long as the robins trill,
Let us taunt old Care with a merry air,
And sing in the face of ill.

Paul Laurence Dunbar (1872–1906)

7TH JULY

A Bird Came Down the Walk

A Bird came down the Walk –
He did not know I saw –
He bit an Angleworm in halves
And ate the fellow, raw,

And then, he drank a Dew
From a convenient Grass –
And then hopped sidewise to the Wall
To let a Beetle pass –

He glanced with rapid eyes,
That hurried all abroad –
They looked like frightened Beads, I thought,
He stirred his Velvet Head

Like one in danger, Cautious,
I offered him a Crumb,
And he unrolled his feathers,
And rowed him softer Home –

Than Oars divide the Ocean,
Too silver for a seam,
Or Butterflies, off Banks of Noon,
Leap, plashless as they swim.

Emily Dickinson (1830–1886)

8TH JULY

Evening Rain

What is lovelier than rain that lingers
Falling through the western light?
The light that's red between my fingers
Bathes infinite heaven's remotest height.

Whither will the cloud its darkness carry
Whose trembling drops about me spill?
Two worlds, of shadow and splendour, marry:
I stand between them rapt and still.

Laurence Binyon (1869–1943)

9TH JULY

The Glow-Worm

TRANSLATED BY WILLIAM COWPER

VERSES 1–5

Beneath the hedge or near the stream,
   A worm is known to stray,
That shows by night a lucid beam,
   Which disappears by day.

Disputes have been and still prevail
   From whence his rays proceed;
Some give that honour to his tail,
   And others to his head.

But this is sure, – the hand of might
   That kindles up the skies,
Gives *him* a modicum of light,
   Proportion'd to his size.

Perhaps indulgent nature meant
   By such a lamp bestow'd,
To bid the trav'ler, as he went,
   Be careful where he trod;

Nor crush a worm, whose useful light
   Might serve, however small,
To show a stumbling stone by night,
   And save him from a fall.

Vincent Bourne (1695–1747)

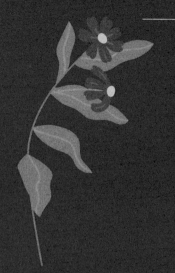

10TH JULY

Sonnet to the River Otter

Dear native Brook! wild Streamlet of the West!
  How many various-fated years have past,
    What happy and what mournful hours, since last
I skimm'd the smooth thin stone along thy breast,
Numbering its light leaps! yet so deep imprest
Sink the sweet scenes of childhood, that mine eyes
  I never shut amid the sunny ray,
But straight with all their tints thy waters rise,
  Thy crossing plank, thy marge with willows grey,
And bedded sand that, vein'd with various dyes
Gleam'd through thy bright transparence! On my way,
  Visions of Childhood! oft have ye beguil'd
Lone manhood's cares, yet waking fondest sighs:
  Ah! that once more I were a careless Child!

Samuel Taylor Coleridge (1772–1834)

11ᵀᴴ JULY

The World Below the Brine

The world below the brine,
Forests at the bottom of the sea, the branches
  and leaves,
Sea-lettuce, vast lichens, strange flowers and
  seeds, the thick tangle, openings, and pink turf,
Different colors, pale gray and green, purple,
  white, and gold, the play of light through the water,
Dumb swimmers there among the rocks, coral, gluten,
  grass, rushes, and the aliment of the swimmers,
Sluggish existences grazing there suspended, or
  slowly crawling close to the bottom,
The sperm-whale at the surface blowing air and
  spray, or disporting with his flukes,
The leaden-eyed shark, the walrus, the turtle, the
  hairy sea-leopard, and the sting-ray,
Passions there, wars, pursuits, tribes, sight in those
  ocean-depths, breathing that thick-breathing air,
    as so many do,
The change thence to the sight here, and to the
  subtle air breathed by beings like us who walk
    this sphere,
The change onward from ours to that of beings
  who walk other spheres.

Walt Whitman (1819–1892)

12TH JULY

Epithalamion

LINES 1–13

Hark, hearer, hear what I do; lend a thought now,
    make believe
We are leaf-whelmed somewhere with the hood
Of some branchy bunchy bushybowered wood,
Southern dene or Lancashire clough or Devon
    cleave,
That leans along the loins of hills, where a
    candycoloured, where a gluegold-brown
Marbled river, boisterously beautiful, between
Roots and rocks is danced and dandled, all in
    froth and waterblowballs, down.
We are there, when we hear a shout
That the hanging honeysuck, the dogeared
    hazels in the cover
Makes dither, makes hover
And the riot of a rout
Of, it must be, boys from the town
Bathing: it is summer's sovereign good.

Gerard Manley Hopkins (1844–1889)

13TH JULY

Flower in the Crannied Wall

Flower in the crannied wall,
I pluck you out of the crannies,
I hold you here, root and all, in my hand,
Little flower – but if I could understand
What you are, root and all, all in all,
I should know what God and man is.

Alfred, Lord Tennyson (1809–1892)

14TH JULY

You Spotted Snakes With Double Tongue

FROM *A MIDSUMMER NIGHT'S DREAM*, ACT II, SCENE II

You spotted snakes with double tongue,
   Thorny hedgehogs, be not seen;
Newts and blind-worms, do no wrong;
   Come not near our Fairy Queen.

   Philomel, with melody,
   Sing in our sweet lullaby;
Lulla, lulla, lullaby; lulla, lulla, lullaby!
     Never harm
     Nor spell nor charm
   Come our lovely lady nigh
   So good night, with lullaby.

Weaving spiders, come not here;
   Hence, you long-legged spinners, hence;
Beetles black, approach not near;
   Worm nor snail do no offence.

Philomel, with melody,
    Sing in our sweet lullaby;
Lulla, lulla, lullaby; lulla, lulla, lullaby!
        Never harm
        Nor spell nor charm
    Come our lovely lady nigh
    So good night, with lullaby.

William Shakespeare (1564–1616)

15ᵀᴴ JULY

The Rainy Summer

There's much afoot in heaven and earth this year;
  The winds hunt up the sun, hunt up the moon,
Trouble the dubious dawn, hasten the drear
  Height of a threatening noon.

No breath of boughs, no breath of leaves, of fronds,
  May linger or grow warm; the trees are loud;
The forest, rooted, tosses in her bonds,
  And strains against the cloud.

No scents may pause within the garden-fold;
  The rifled flowers are cold as ocean-shells;
Bees, humming in the storm, carry their cold
  Wild honey to cold cells.

Alice Meynell (1847–1922)

16TH JULY

Nocturne

Day, like a flower of gold fades on its crimson bed;
For the many chambered night unbars to shut its
    sweetness up;
From earth and heaven fast drawn together a
    heavy stillness is shed,
And our hearts drink the shadowy splendour
    from a brimming cup.

For the indrawn breath of beauty thrills the holy
    caves of night;
Shimmering winds of heaven fall gently and
    mysterious hands caress
Our wan brows with cooling rapture of the
    delicate starlight
Dropping from the night's blue walls in endless
    veils of loveliness.

Isaac Rosenberg (1890–1918)

17TH JULY

Little Birds of the Night

Little birds of the night
Aye, they have much to tell
Perching there in rows
Blinking at me with their serious eyes
Recounting of flowers they have seen and loved
Of meadows and groves of the distance
And pale sands at the foot of the sea
And breezes that fly in the leaves.
They are vast in experience
These little birds that come in the night.

Stephen Crane (1871–1900)

18TH JULY

A Cat's Conscience

A dog will often steal a bone,
But conscience lets him not alone,
And by his tail his guilt is known.

But cats consider theft a game,
And, howsoever you may blame,
Refuse the slightest sign of shame.

When food mysteriously goes,
The chances are that Pussy knows
More than she leads you to suppose.

And hence there is no need for you,
If Puss declines a meal or to,
To feel her pulse and make ado.

Anon

19TH JULY

Deer

Shy in their herding dwell the fallow deer.
They are spirits of wild sense. Nobody near
Comes upon their pastures. There a life they live,
Of sufficient beauty, phantom, fugitive,
Treading as in jungles free leopards do,
Printless as evelight, instant as dew.
The great kine are patient, and home-coming sheep
Know our bidding. The fallow deer keep
Delicate and far their counsels wild,
Never to be folded reconciled
To the spoiling hand as the poor flocks are;
Lightfoot, and swift, and unfamiliar,
These you may not hinder, unconfined
Beautiful flocks of the mind.

John Drinkwater (1882–1937)

20ᵀᴴ JULY

At Night

The wind is singing through the trees to-night,
  A deep-voiced song of rushing cadences
  And crashing intervals. No summer breeze
Is this, though hot July is at its height,
Gone is her gentler music; with delight
  She listens to this booming like the seas,
  These elemental, loud necessities
Which call to her to answer their swift might.
  Above the tossing trees shines down a star,
  Quietly bright; this wild, tumultuous joy
Quickens nor dims its splendour. And my mind,
  O Star! is filled with your white light, from far,
  So suffer me this one night to enjoy
The freedom of the onward sweeping wind.

Amy Lowell (1874–1925)

21ˢᵗ JULY

On a Drop of Dew

LINES 1–18

See how the Orient Dew,
  Shed from the Bosom of the Morn
  Into the blowing Roses,
Yet careless of its Mansion new
For the clear Region where 'twas born,
  Round in its self incloses:
  And in its little Globes Extent,
Frames as it can its native Element.
  How it the purple flow'r does slight,
    Scarce touching where it lyes,
But gazing back upon the Skies,
  Shines with a mournful Light,
    Like its own Tear,
Because so long divided from the Sphear.
  Restless it roules and unsecure,
    Trembling lest it grow impure,
  Till the warm Sun pitty it's Pain,
And to the Skies exhale it back again.

Andrew Marvell (1621–1678)

22ᴺᴰ JULY

The River God's Song

FROM THE FAITHFUL SHEPHERDESS

Do not fear to put thy feet
Naked in the river, sweet
Think not leach or newt or toad
Will bite thy foot when thou hast trod;
Nor let the water rising high,
As thou wadest in, make thee cry
And sob; but ever live with me,
And not a wave shall trouble thee.

John Fletcher (1579–1625)

23RD JULY

Trees in the Garden

Ah in the thunder air
how still the trees are!

And the lime-tree, lovely and tall, every leaf silent
hardly looses even a last breath of perfume.

And the ghostly, creamy coloured little tree of leaves
white, ivory white among the rambling greens
how evanescent, variegated elder, she hesitates on
the green grass as if, in another moment, she
    would disappear
with all her grace of foam!

And the larch that is only a column, it goes up
    too tall to see:
and the balsam-pines that are blue with the grey-
    blue blueness of things from the sea,
and the young copper beech, its leaves red-rosey
    at the ends
how still they are together, they stand so still
in the thunder air, all strangers to one another
as the green grass glows upwards, strangers in
    the garden.

D. H. Lawrence (1885–1930)

24TH JULY

The Woodpecker

I once a King and chief
Now am the tree-bark's thief,
Ever 'twixt trunk and leaf
Chasing the prey.

William Morris (1834–1896)

25TH JULY

Among the Firs

And what a charm is in the rich hot scent
  Of old fir forests heated by the sun,
  Where drops of resin down the rough bark run,
And needle litter breathes its wonderment.

The old fir forests heated by the sun,
  Their thought shall linger like the lingering scent,
  Their beauty haunt us, and a wonderment
Of moss, of fern, of cones, of rills that run.

The needle litter breathes a wonderment;
  The crimson crans are sparkling in the sun;
  From tree to tree the scampering squirrels run;
The hum of insects blends with heat and scent.

The drops of resin down the rough bark run;
  And riper, ever riper, grows the scent;
  But eve has come, to end the wonderment,
And slowly up the tree trunk climbs the sun.

Eugene Lee-Hamilton (1845–1907)

26TH JULY

The Grasshopper

O thou that swingst upon the waving hair
  Of some well-fillèd oaten beard,
Drunk every night with a delicious tear
  Dropped thee from heaven, where now th' art reared;

The joys of earth and air are thine entire,
  That with thy feet and wings dost hop and fly;
And when thy poppy works thou dost retire
  To thy carved acorn bed to lie.

Up with the day, the sun thou welcom'st then,
  Sportst in the gilt plats of his beams,
And all these merry days mak'st merry men,
  Thyself, and melancholy streams.

Richard Lovelace (1618–1657)

27TH **JULY**

The Bothie of Tober-Na-Vuolich

PART III, LINES 19–46

There is a stream, I name not its name, lest
  inquisitive tourist
Hunt it, and make it a lion, and get it at last into
  guide-books,
Springing far off from a loch unexplored in the
  folds of great mountains,
Falling two miles through rowan and stunted
  alder, enveloped
Then for four more in a forest of pine, where
  broad and ample
Spreads, to convey it, the glen with heathery
  slopes on both sides:
Broad and fair the stream, with occasional falls
  and narrows;
But, where the glen of its course approaches the
  vale of the river,
Met and blocked by a huge interposing mass of
  granite,
Scarce by a channel deep-cut, raging up, and
  raging onward,
Forces its flood through a passage so narrow a
  lady would step it.

There, across the great rocky wharves, a wooden
    bridge goes,
Carrying a path to the forest; below, three
    hundred yards, say,
Lower in level some twenty-five feet, through
    flats of shingle,
Stepping-stones and a cart-track cross in the
    open valley.
But in the interval here the boiling, pent-up water
Frees itself by a final descent, attaining a basin,
Ten feet wide and eighteen long, with whiteness
    and fury
Occupied partly, but mostly pellucid, pure, a
    mirror;
Beautiful there for the colour derived from green
    rocks under;

Beautiful, most of all, where beads of foam
   uprising
Mingle their clouds of white with the delicate
   hue of the stillness.
Cliff over cliff for its sides, with rowan and
   pendent birch boughs,
Here it lies, unthought of above at the bridge and
   pathway,
Still more enclosed from below by wood and rocky
   projection.
You are shut in, left alone with yourself and
   perfection of water,
Hid on all sides, left alone with yourself and the
   goddess of bathing.

Arthur Hugh Clough (1819–1861)

28TH JULY

The Hairy Dog

My dog's so furry I've not seen
His face for years and years;
His eyes are buried out of sight,
I only guess his ears.

When people ask me for his breed,
I do not know or care;
He has the beauty of them all
Hidden beneath his hair.

Herbert Asquith (1881–1947)

29TH JULY

Where Innocent Bright-eyed Daisies Are

Where innocent bright-eyed daisies are,
   With blades of grass between,
Each daisy stands up like a star
   Out of a sky of green.

Christina Rossetti (1830–1894)

30ᵀᴴ JULY

Impressions II

LA FUITE DE LA LUNE

To outer senses there is peace,
A dreamy peace on either hand,
Deep silence in the shadowy land,
Deep silence where the shadows cease.

Save for a cry that echoes shrill
From some lone bird disconsolate;
A corncrake calling to its mate;
The answer from the misty hill.

And suddenly the moon withdraws
Her sickle from the lightening skies,
And to her sombre cavern flies,
Wrapped in a veil of yellow gauze.

Oscar Wilde (1854–1900)

31ˢᵗ JULY

Haze

Woof of the sun, ethereal gauze,
Woven of Nature's richest stuffs,
Visible heat, air-water, and dry sea,
Last conquest of the eye;
Toil of the day displayed, sun-dust,
Aerial surf upon the shores of earth,
Ethereal estuary, frith of light,
Breakers of air, billows of heat,
Fine summer spray on inland seas;
Bird of the sun, transparent-winged,
Owlet of noon, soft-pinioned,
From heath or stubble rising without song;
Establish thy serenity o'er the fields.

Henry David Thoreau (1817–1862)

AUGUST

Now Fades the Glimmering Landscape

1ST AUGUST

Sounds in the Wood

Trees breathe
Quiet in the wood.
Winds hush
Cradled in the branches.
Jays squall
Carping in the startled tree-tops.
Tits pipe
Keen in the secret, the secret thicket.

Mavis Pilbeam (1946–)

2ND AUGUST

Audley Court

But ere the night we rose
And saunter'd home beneath a moon, that, just
In crescent, dimly rain'd about the leaf
Twilights of airy silver, till we reach'd
The limit of the hills; and as we sank
From rock to rock upon the glooming quay,
The town was hush'd beneath us: lower down
The bay was oily calm; the harbour-buoy,
Sole star of phosphorescence in the calm,
With one green sparkle ever and anon
Dipt by itself, and we were glad at heart.

Alfred, Lord Tennyson (1809–1892)

3RD AUGUST

Summer Rain

Thick lay the dust, uncomfortably white,
In glaring mimicry of Arab sands.
The woods and mountains slept in hazy light;
The meadows look'd athirst and tawny tann'd;
The little rills had left their channels bare.
With scarce a pool to witness what they were;
And the shrunk river gleam'd 'mid oozy stones.
That stared like any famish'd giant's bones.

Sudden the hills grew black, and hot as stove
The air beneath; it was a toil to be.
There was a growling as of angry Jove,
Provoked by Juno's prying jealousy –
A flash – a crash – the firmament was split.
And down it came in drops – the smallest fit
To drown a bee in fox-glove bell conceal'd;
Joy fill'd the brook, and comfort cheer'd the field.

Hartley Coleridge (1796–1849)

4TH AUGUST

No Matter

water laps grindingly dark on a lip
of teeming sand (worms/lost coins) &
those gathered (bodies weighted by
sleep) have little need for the torrent of
stars or the names of planets: limbs
containing bones at rest.

Joel Knight (1975–)

5TH AUGUST

On Craig Ddu

FROM *INTERMEZZO: PASTORAL*

The sky through the leaves of the bracken,
Tenderly, pallidly blue,
Nothing but sky as I lie on the mountain-top.
Hark! for the wind as it blew,

Rustling the tufts of my bracken above me,
Brought from below
Into the silence the sound of the water.
Hark! for the oxen low,

Sheep are bleating, a dog
Barks, at a farm in the vale:
Blue, through the bracken, softly enveloping
Silence, a veil.

Arthur Symons (1865–1945)

6TH AUGUST

The Rose

O Rose, thou art the flower of flowers, thou
    fragrant wonder,
  Who shall describe thee in they ruddy prime,
Thy perfect fulness in the summer time,
  When the pale leaves blushingly part asunder
And show the warm red heart lies glowing under?
  Thou shouldst bloom surely in some sunny clime,
Untouched by blights and chilly Winter's rime,
  Where lightnings never flash nor peals the thunder.
And yet in happier spheres they cannot need thee
  So much as we do with our weight of woe;
Perhaps they would not tend, perhaps not heed thee,
  And thou wouldst lonely and neglected grow;
And He Who is All-Wise, He hath decreed thee
  To gladden earth and cheer all hearts below.

Christina Rossetti (1830–1894)

7ᵀᴴ AUGUST

In the Water

FROM *A MIDSUMMER HOLIDAY*

VERSE 1

The sea is awake, and the sound of the song
   of the joy of her waking is rolled
From afar to the star that recedes, from anear
   to the wastes of the wild wide shore.
Her call is a trumpet compelling us homeward:
   if dawn in her east be acold,
From the sea shall we crave not her grace to rekindle
   the life that it kindled before,
Her breath to requicken, her bosom to rock us,
   her kisses to bless as of yore?
For the wind, with his wings half open, at pause
   in the sky, neither fettered nor free,
Leans waveward and flutters the ripple to laughter
   and fain would the twain of us be
Where lightly the wave yearns forward from under
   the curve of the deep dawn's dome,
And, full of the morning and fired with the pride
   of the glory thereof and the glee,
Strike out from the shore as the heart in us bids
   and beseeches, athirst for the foam.

Algernon Charles Swinburne (1837–1909)

8TH AUGUST

Kingfisher

Dropping
Like a splinter from the sky
It knives the water,
Swiftly strikes,
Turns, surges
Up through the splattering surface,
Back to the willow branch,
Where it sits triumphant,
Wet feathers glistening,
Its silver catch
Dangling from its beak.

John Foster (1941–)

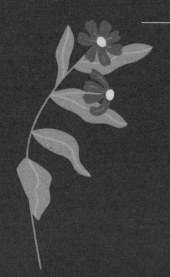

9ᵀᴴ AUGUST

Ah! Sun-Flower

FROM *SONGS OF EXPERIENCE*

Ah, Sun-flower! weary of time,
Who countest the steps of the sun,
Seeking after that sweet golden clime
Where the traveller's journey is done.

Where the Youth pined away with desire,
And the pale Virgin shrouded in snow:
Arise from their graves, and aspire,
Where my Sun-flower wishes to go.

William Blake (1757–1827)

10TH AUGUST

The Ousel Cock

FROM *A MIDSUMMER'S NIGHT DREAM*, ACT III, SCENE I

The ousel cock, so black of hue,
    With orange-tawny bill;
The throstle with his note so true,
    The wren with little quill.

The finch, the sparrow, and the lark,
    The plainsong cuckoo grey,
Whose note full many a man doth mark,
    And dares not answer 'Nay'.

William Shakespeare (1564–1616)

11ᵀᴴ AUGUST

The Estuary

A light elegant wall waves down
The riverside, for tidiness
Or decoration – this water
Needs little keeping in – but turns
The corner to face the ocean
And thickens to a bastion.

No one can really taste or smell
Where the salt starts but at one point
The first building looks out to sea
And the two sides of the river
Are forced apart by cold light
And wind and different grasses.

I see this now, but at one time
I had to believe that the two
Sides were almost identical.
I was a child who dared not seem
Gloomy. Traversing grey water
From the east side where I was born

And had spent a normal cross life,
To live gratefully with strangers
On the west side, I grinned and clowned.
I did not go back for ages
And became known for cheerfulness
In a house where all was not well.

Grief was a poltergeist that would
Not materialize but broke
Everything. Neither believed in
Nor dreaded, it took one decade
To appear, one to be recognized,
Then cleared the air wonderfully

So that nowadays I am able
To see the estuary as two
Distinct pieces of countryside,
Not a great deal to choose between
Them perhaps but at least different,
Rising normally from two roots.

On one bank, stiff fields of corn grow
To the hilltop, are draped over
It surrealistically.
On the other, little white boats
Sag sideways twice every day
As the sea pulls away their prop.

Patricia Beer (1919–1999)

12TH AUGUST

Drawing Near the Light

Lo, when we wade the tangled wood,
In haste and hurry to be there,
Nought seem its leaves and blossoms good,
For all that they be fashioned fair.

But looking up, at last we see
The glimmer of the open light,
From o'er the place where we would be:
Then grow the very brambles bright.

So now, amidst our day of strife,
With many a matter glad we play,
When once we see the light of life
Gleam through the tangle of to-day.

William Morris (1834–1896)

13TH AUGUST

Elegy Written in a Country Churchyard

The curfew tolls the knell of parting day,
The lowing herd wind slowly o'er the lea,
The plowman homeward plods his weary way,
And leaves the world to darkness and to me.

Now fades the glimmering landscape on the sight,
And all the air a solemn stillness holds,
Save where the beetle wheels his droning flight,
And drowsy tinklings lull the distant folds;

Save that from yonder ivy-mantled tow'r
The moping owl does to the moon complain
Of such, as wand'ring near her secret bow'r,
Molest her ancient solitary reign.

Beneath those rugged elms, that yew-tree's shade,
Where heaves the turf in many a mould'ring heap,
Each in his narrow cell for ever laid,
The rude Forefathers of the hamlet sleep.

The breezy call of incense-breathing Morn,
The swallow twitt'ring from the straw-built shed,
The cock's shrill clarion, or the echoing horn,
No more shall rouse them from their lowly bed.

For them no more the blazing hearth shall burn,
Or busy housewife ply her evening care:
No children run to lisp their sire's return,
Or climb his knees the envied kiss to share.

Oft did the harvest to their sickle yield,
Their furrow oft the stubborn glebe has broke;
How jocund did they drive their team afield!
How bow'd the woods beneath their sturdy stroke!

Let not Ambition mock their useful toil,
Their homely joys, and destiny obscure;
Nor Grandeur hear with a disdainful smile,
The short and simple annals of the poor.

The boast of heraldry, the pomp of power,
And all that beauty, all that wealth e'er gave,
Await alike the inevitable hour.
The paths of glory lead but to the grave.

Thomas Gray (1716–1771)

14TH AUGUST

Twilight (III)

A sumptuous splendour of leaves
Murmurously fanning the evening heaven;
And I hear
In the soft living grey shadows,
In the brooding evanescent atmosphere,
The voice of impatient night.

The splendour shall vanish in a vaster splendour;
Its own identity shall lose itself,
And the golden glory of day
Give birth to the glimmering face of the twilight,
And she shall grow into a vast enormous pearl maiden
Whose velvet tresses shall envelop the world –
Night.

Isaac Rosenberg (1890–1918)

15TH AUGUST

To a Daisy

Slight as thou art, thou art enough to hide,
  Like all created things, secrets from me,
  And stand a barrier to eternity.
And I, how can I praise thee well and wide
From where I dwell – upon the hither side?
  Thou little veil for so great mystery,
  When shall I penetrate all things and thee,
And then look back? For this I must abide,

Till thou shalt grow and fold and be unfurled
Literally between me and the world.
  Then I shall drink from in beneath a spring,
And from a poet's side shall read his book.
O daisy mine, what will it be to look
  From God's side even of such a simple thing?

Alice Meynell (1847–1922)

16TH AUGUST

The Sea-bird's Cry

'Tis harsh to hear, from ledge or peak,
The sunny cormorant's tuneless shriek;
Fierce songs they chant, in pool or cave,
Dark wanderers of the western wave.
Here will the listening landsman pray
For memory's music, far away;
Soft throats that nestling by the rose,
Soothe the glad rivulet as it flows.

Cease, stranger! cease that fruitless word,
Give eve's hushed bough to woodland bird:
Let the winged minstrel's valley-note
'Mid flowers and fragrance, pause and float.
Here must the echoing beak prevail,
To pierce the storm and cleave the gale;
To call, when warring tides shall foam,
The fledgeling of the waters home.

Wild things are here of sea and land,
Stern surges and a haughty strand;
Sea-monsters haunt yon caverned lair,
The mermaid wrings her briny hair.
That cry, those sullen accents sound
Like native echoes of the ground.
Lo! He did all things well Who gave
The sea-bird's voice to such a wave.

Rev. Robert Stephen Hawker, Vicar of Morwenstow (1803–1875)

17TH AUGUST

Bonie Doon

Ye flowery banks o' bonie Doon,
  How can ye blume sae fair?
How can ye chant, ye little birds,
  And I sae fu' o' care?

Thou'll break my heart, thou bonie bird,
  That sings upon the bough;
Thou minds me o' the happy days,
  When my fause luve was true.

Thou'll break my heart, thou bonie bird,
  That sings beside thy mate;
For sae I sat, and sae I sang,
  And wist na o' my fate.

Aft hae I roved by bonie Doon
  To see the wood-bine twine,
And ilka bird sang o' its luve,
  And sae did I o' mine.

Wi' lightsome heart I pu'd a rose
 Frae aff its thorny tree;
And my fause luver staw my rose
 But left the thorn wi' me.

Robert Burns (1759–1796)

18TH AUGUST

The Bat

The Bat is dun, with wrinkled Wings –
Like fallow Article –
And not a song pervade his Lips –
Or none perceptible.

His small Umbrella quaintly halved
Describing in the Air
An Arc alike inscrutable
Elate Philosopher.

Deputed from what Firmament –
Of what Astute Abode –
Empowered with what Malignity
Auspiciously withheld –

To his adroit Creator
Ascribe no less the praise –
Beneficent, believe me,
His Eccentricities –

Emily Dickinson (1830–1886)

19TH AUGUST

An August Midnight

I

A shaded lamp and a waving blind,
And the beat of a clock from a distant floor:
On this scene enter – winged, horned, and spined –
A longlegs, a moth, and a dumbledore;
While 'mid my page there idly stands
A sleepy fly, that rubs its hands ...

II

Thus meet we five, in this still place,
At this point of time, at this point in space.
– My guests besmear my new-penned line,
Or bang at the lamp and fall supine.
'God's humblest, they!' I muse. Yet why?
They know Earth-secrets that know not I.

Thomas Hardy (1840–1928)

20ᵗʰ AUGUST

The Butterfly Trainers

Butterflies didn't always know
How to spread their wings and go
Gliding down the slopes of air
On their spangled wings and fair;
Never dared to leave the land
Till the elves took them in hand,
Made them bridle, bit and reins
Out of shiny corn silk skeins;
Drove them through the long blue hours,
Introducing them to Flowers.

Rachel Field (1894–1942)

21ˢᵀ AUGUST

The Silver Mist More Lowly Swims

The silver mist more lowly swims
And each green bosomed valley dims
And o'er the neighbouring meadow lies
Like half seen visions by dim eyes
Green trees look grey, bright waters black
The lated crow has lost her track
And flies by guess her journey home

She flops along and cannot see
Her peaceful nest on odlin tree
The lark drops down and cannot meet
The taller black grown clumps of wheat
The mists that rise from heat of day
Fades fields and meadows all away

John Clare (1793–1864)

22ND AUGUST

The Dor-Hawk

Fern-owl, Churn-owl, or Goat-sucker,
   Night-jar, Dor-hawk, or whate'er
Be thy name among a dozen, –
Whip-poor-Will's and Who-are-you's cousin,
Chuck-Will's-widow's near relation,
Thou art at thy night vocation,
   Thrilling the still evening air!

In the dark brown wood beyond us,
   Where the night lies dusk and deep;
Where the fox his burrow maketh,
Where the tawny owl awaketh
   Nightly from his day-long sleep;

There Dor-hawk is thy abiding,
   Meadow green is not for thee;
While the aspen branches shiver,
'Mid the roaring of the river,
   Comes thy chirring voice to me.

Bird, thy form I never looked on,
   And to see it do not care;
Thou hast been, and thou art only
As a voice of forests lonely,
   Heard and dwelling only there.

Bringing thoughts of dusk and shadow;
   Trees huge-branched in ceaseless change;
Pallid night-moths, spectre-seeming;
All a silent land of dreaming,
   Indistinct and large and strange.

Mary Howitt (1799–1888)

23RD AUGUST

I Know a Bank Where the Wild Thyme Blows

FROM *A MIDSUMMER NIGHT'S DREAM*, ACT II, SCENE I

I know a bank where the wild thyme blows,
Where oxlips and the nodding violet grows,
Quite overcanopied with luscious woodbine,
With sweet musk-roses, and with eglantine:
There sleeps Titania sometime of the night,
Lulled in these flowers with dances and delight.

William Shakespeare (1564–1616)

24TH AUGUST

To a Squirrel at Kyle-na-no

Come play with me;
Why should you run
Through the shaking tree
As though I'd a gun
To strike you dead?
When all I would do
Is to scratch your head
And let you go.

W. B. Yeats (1865–1939)

25TH AUGUST

Meeting at Night

I

The grey sea and the long black land;
And the yellow half-moon large and low;
And the startled little waves that leap
In fiery ringlets from their sleep,
As I gain the cove with pushing prow,
And quench its speed in the slushy sand.

II

Then a mile of warm sea-scented beach;
Three fields to cross till a farm appears;
A tap at the pane, the quick sharp scratch
And blue spurt of a lighted match,
And a voice less loud, thro' its joys and fears,
Than the two hearts beating each to each!

Robert Browning (1812–1889)

26TH AUGUST

Between the Dusk of a Summer Night

PRAELUDIUM, XXII

Between the dusk of a summer night
  And the dawn of a summer day,
We caught at a mood as it passed in flight,
  And we bade it stoop and stay.
And what with the dawn of night began
  With the dusk of day was done;
For that is the way of woman and man,
  When a hazard has made them one.

Arc upon arc, from shade to shine,
  The World went thundering free;
And what was his errand but hers and mine –
  The lords of him, I and she?
O, it's die we must, but it's live we can,
  And the marvel of earth and sun
Is all for the joy of woman and man
  And the longing that makes them one.

W. E. Henley (1849–1903)

27TH AUGUST

On a Wet Summer

All ye who, far from town, in rural hall,
   Like me were wont to dwell near pleasant field,
   Enjoying all the sunny day did yield,
   With me the change lament, in irksome thrall,
By rains incessant held; for now no call
   From early swain invites my hand to wield
   The scythe; in parlour dim I sit concealed,
   And mark the lessening sand from hourglass fall,
Or 'neath my window view the wistful train
   Of dripping poultry, whom the vine's broad leaves
   Shelter no more. – Mute is the mournful plain,
Silent the swallow sits beneath the thatch,
   And vacant hind hangs pensive o'er his hatch,
   Counting the frequent drips from reeded eaves.

John Codrington Bampfylde (1754–1796)

28TH AUGUST

The Yellow-hammer

When, towards the summer's close,
   Lanes are dry,
And unclipt the hedgethorn rows,
   There we fly!

While the harvest waggons pass
   With their load,
Shedding corn upon the grass
   By the road,

In a flock we follow them,
   On and on,
Seize a wheat-ear by the stem,
   And are gone ...

With our funny little song,
   Thus you may
Often see us flit along,
   Day by day.

Thomas Hardy (1840–1928)

29TH AUGUST

A Story of the Sea-Shore

INTRODUCTION, LINES 1–6

I sought the long clear twilights of my home,
Far in the pale-blue skies and slaty seas,
What time the sunset dies not utterly,
But withered to a ghost-like stealthy gleam,
Round the horizon creeps the short-lived night,
And changes into sunrise in a swoon.

George MacDonald (1824–1905)

30ᵗʰ AUGUST

The Things That Grow

It was nothing but a little neglected garden,
Laurel-screened, and hushed in a hot stillness;
An old pear-tree, and flowers mingled with weeds.
Yet as I came to it all unawares, it seemed
Charged with mystery; and I stopped, intruding,
Fearful of hurting that so absorbed stillness.
For I was tingling with the wind's salty splendour,
And still my senses moved with the keel's buoyance
Out on the water, where strong light was shivered
Into a dance dazzling as drops of flame.
The rocking radiance and the winged sail's lifting
And the noise of the rush of the water left behind
Sang to my body of movement, victory, joy.
But here the light was asleep, and green, green
In a veined leaf it glowed among the shadows.
A hollyhock rose to the sun and bathed its flowers

Luminously clustered in the unmoving air;
A butterfly lazily winked its gorgeous wings;
Marigolds burned intently amid the grass;
The ripening pears hung each with a rounded shadow:
All beyond was drowned in the indolent blueness;
And at my feet, like a word of an unknown tongue,
Was the midnight-dark bloom of the delicate pansy.
Suddenly these things awed my heart, as if here
In perishing blossom and springing shoot were a power
Greater than shipwrecking winds and all wild waters.

Laurence Binyon (1869–1943)

31ST AUGUST

Who Has Seen the Wind?

Who has seen the wind?
  Neither I nor you:
But when the leaves hang trembling,
  The wind is passing thro'.

Who has seen the wind?
  Neither you nor I:
But when the trees bow down their heads,
  The wind is passing by.

Christina Rossetti (1830–1894)

Index of first lines

Index of poets

Acknowledgements

As always, a huge thanks to everyone at Hatchards in Piccadilly, St Pancras and Cheltenham for looking after my books so well.

Thanks to all my friends who made recommendations, and Nicola Newman and my wonderful editors at Batsford.

For curious readers, Matilda is a small, grey tabby cat, who went missing in late autumn when I was compiling the original anthology from which this collection is taken. She was found in spring and that first summer, and ever since, she has sought the warmth of every ray of sunshine. Without Mat and Sarah it would have been a much harder time.

Sources

David Austin, 'The Sea By Moonlight', from
The Breathing Earth, Enitharmon Press, 2014.
Reprinted with permission of David Austin Roses.

Patricia Beer, 'The Estuary', from *Patricia Beer:
Collected Poems*, Carcanet Press, 1990. Reprinted
by permission of Carcanet Press Limited.

Edmund Blunden, 'A Waterpiece', from *Edmund
Blunden: Selected Poems*, Carcanet Press, 1982.
Reprinted by permission of Carcanet Press
Limited.

John Foster, 'Kingfisher', from *The Poetry Chest*, Oxford University Press, 2007. Reproduced with permission of the Licensor through PLSClear.

Joel Knight, 'No Matter'. With kind permission of Joel Knight.

Mavis Pilbeam, 'Sounds in the Wood', from *Birds*, British Museum Press, 2015. Reprinted with permission of Mavis Pilbeam.